How to Build an In-Law Unit in California

YOUR ESSENTIAL GUIDE

Second Edition

Updated with the new 2020 ADU laws.

Ron Chin

INSPIRE PRESS
Sacramento, CA

HOW TO BUILD AN IN-LAW UNIT IN CALIFORNIA
YOUR ESSENTIAL GUIDE
Second Edition: Updated with the new 2020 ADU laws.

ISBN-13: 978-1-938196-18-8

Inspire Press, PO Box 276794, Sacramento, CA 95827, USA
http://inspirewriters.com

Cover photo by Julie Williams, ©2018, 2020. All rights reserved.
Architectural drawings used by permission of Walker CAD Design

Printed in United States of America

D DEDICATION

To my mother, Victoria

TABLE OF CONTENTS

(A) ACKNOWLEDGEMENTS

I thank God for opening the door for us to buy our house so that we could build an in-law unit for my mother. I also would like to thank my writer's critique group from Inspire Christian Writers for providing feedback.

① INTRODUCTION

As the new year began in 2017, my wife Jill and I had no plans to change our housing situation. We had been renting a townhouse in Fremont, California for almost four years, and the rent was reasonable, at least by Silicon Valley standards. Although we wanted to buy a house, it didn't seem possible because of the rising home prices in Fremont and our financial situation. We had a good chunk of money in the bank from the sale of our last home, and Jill's piano teaching business was doing well, but we didn't have very high income because I only had a part-time job.

On January 11, 2017, I received a call that would alter the direction of our lives significantly. The property management company which managed our rented townhouse called and informed me that the owner had decided to sell the townhouse. As a result, we needed to make a rather quick decision about our housing situation. For us, it was very important because our house was not just our residence; it was also the location of Jill's business. Jill taught piano lessons in the townhouse.

Also, we had another matter to consider—taking care of my mother, who was in her 80s and was living by herself in a large house in the Berkeley area, about 40 miles from Fremont. She had lost a lot of her hearing, which made it difficult to communicate with her over the phone. She was still relatively healthy, but from time to time, she would have a physical ailment, and we did not live close enough to help her. Therefore, Jill and I felt that it might be a mutually beneficial situation if we combined resources with my mother to buy a house, and my mother lived with us.

We approached my mother with the idea, and she was open to purchasing a house together. She told us that the ideal situation would be if she could have an in-law unit that was not in a separate building from the main house. She wanted to have the security of living in the same house, but at the same time wanted to have her own living space and independence. With the addition of some financial resources from my mother, we felt that it was possible to find a single-family house in Fremont that could be renovated to meet our needs.

I decided to contact the real estate agent who had helped me to sell my first house in Fremont. I had spoken with him about four years previously, and he believed that instead of buying a move-in ready house, it was better financially to buy an older property and renovate it. For these kinds of houses, my real estate agent partnered with a contractor who would renovate the properties that my real estate agent helped his clients to purchase.

My real estate agent showed us several different houses, but it was difficult to purchase a house because the real estate market was very hot, and most houses were sold for well over the asking price. However, one day, I saw a house for sale on the internet, and Jill and I went to go see it. When we arrived at the house, there wasn't a "For Sale" sign in front of the house, so I texted my real estate agent to ask if it was really for sale. After doing some investigation, my real estate agent found out that the house was for sale, but the seller's agent apparently wasn't putting much effort into selling it. On top of that, the seller's agent, who was based in San Jose, did not list the house on the Multiple Listing Service (MLS) where Fremont homes were typically listed. Therefore, most real estate agents in Fremont did not know that this house was for sale. Less competition!

We met my real estate agent at the house, which clearly needed some renovation. When we walked into the two-story house, I thought it was kind of strange because the first floor had two main rooms—a small office in the front of the house and a large bedroom with a bathroom in the back of the house. The kitchen, living room and three other bedrooms were upstairs. However, Jill pointed out that this would be a good house for our needs. On the first floor, the large bedroom with a bathroom could be converted into an in-law unit, and the small office could be used for her piano studio. On the second floor, there could be a living space for me and Jill. We put in an offer the next day, and because there wasn't much competition, we were able to get the house for only $10,000 over the asking price. We felt that it was divine providence that allowed us to get this house!

On March 15, 2017, we completed the purchase of the house, which had 4 bedrooms, 2 bathrooms and 1,722 square feet. We began to make plans with our contractor about the renovation. At that time, all of us were unaware of the new in-law unit legislation in the state of California that went into effect at the beginning of 2017. These new laws encouraged the construction of in-law units.

The California State Legislature had recognized the housing

shortage in the state and determined that accessory dwelling units (ADUs), the formal name for in-law units, were a beneficial type of residence that could help mitigate the problem. The state passed three laws effective on January 1, 2017 that reduced some barriers to building ADUs and allowed the construction of a special type of ADU – a junior accessory dwelling unit (JADU). The JADU was the type of unit that we were going to build for my mother's in-law unit! Without this new law, we would not have been able to build a kitchen in the in-law unit because local laws typically prohibited having two kitchens in the same house.

When we started the renovation in early May, we thought that the in-law unit would be completed in a few months. However, as with many renovations, it took much longer than expected. We ran into a multitude of problems which slowed the progress on our project. Finally, after about seven and a half months, we received a nice Christmas present when the in-law unit became habitable before Christmas Day, 2017.

During the process, I learned a lot about building an in-law unit. If we had known at the beginning of the process what we know now, it would have made the process much easier. I would like to share our story and the knowledge that we gained so that you will be more informed and can make good decisions if you want to build an in-law unit in California. This second edition of *How to Build an In-Law Unit in California* contains information about the new ADU laws in the state of California that went into effect on January 1, 2020. These laws have made it significantly easier to build an ADU in California. It's a great time for homeowners in California to build an in-law unit!

1 THE BENEFITS & DIFFICULTIES OF BUILDING AN IN-LAW UNIT

I tend to be a planner who carefully researches and thinks through the decisions that I make. When I worked in high-tech, I had a job as a material planner for a computer company. However, when we were looking to buy a house and build an in-law unit, I felt that I was reacting more than I was planning. The housing market was so hot that we had to quickly decide if we wanted to pursue a particular house. Houses rarely stayed on the market more than a week. Also, I didn't realize that the State of California had passed accessory dwelling unit (ADU) laws, and that I should investigate the details about building an in-law unit. Often, we were finding out new information and figuring out solutions as the project went along.

Before a homeowner decides to build an in-law unit, it is helpful to weigh the benefits and difficulties of the project. Basically, homeowners should know what they are getting themselves into! The benefits of building an in-law unit are great, but it is not an easy process. An ADU project has similarities to a home remodel, but there are also some added complexities because of the legal requirements.

In this chapter, we will look at some helpful information for homeowners to know before embarking on an ADU building project. We will start with something that many people probably have not considered—by building an in-law unit, a homeowner is doing something beneficial for the common good.

Benefits for California

Housing is expensive in the major cities in California and their surrounding communities. Although the housing market slowed down in 2019, the median home price in Los Angeles County reached an all-time high of $618,000 in June 2019.[1] The city where I live, Fremont, used to be known for affordable housing. I purchased my first single-family home in Fremont in 1999 for just under $300,000. Zillow reported that the median home value in Fremont in September 2019 was $1,075,500.[2] That's insane! What is the reason for these soaring house prices? It's basic economics—demand is greater than supply. In Northern California, the high-tech boom has created wealth, jobs, and population growth, but construction of new housing has not kept pace with the demand. In Los Angeles County, new construction has lagged for decades. Almost 60 percent of the county's housing was built before 1970.[3]

The State of California now recognizes that part of the solution to the problem is the construction of accessory dwelling units. The California Department of Housing and Community Development states:

> ADUs are a critical form of infill-development that can be affordable and offer important housing choices within existing neighborhoods. ADUs are a powerful type of housing unit because they allow for different uses, and serve different populations ranging from students and young professionals

to young families, people with disabilities and senior citizens. By design, ADUs are more affordable and can provide additional income to homeowners.[4]

The construction of ADUs adds actual housing units. If you visit my property and look at the front of the house, you will see two addresses—one for the main house and one for the ADU. Each ADU has a unique address.

One city in California which already has had success with ADU development is Santa Cruz. The changes in Santa Cruz began with a grass-roots community effort to address the housing shortage in the city. In response to this community effort, the City of Santa Cruz introduced its Accessory Dwelling Unit Development Program in 2003, which simplified the permit process, reduced fees and provided manuals that guided homeowners through the ADU development process.[5]

San Francisco also has taken steps to encourage ADU development. In 2013, the city only allowed ADUs to be built in the Castro neighborhood. Due to San Francisco's restrictive policies, many people had built unpermitted ADUs in prior years. As the city began to recognize the value of ADUs, changes were made to the laws. In May 2014, San Francisco introduced a procedure that allowed unpermitted ADUs to be legalized. Then, in 2016, the city decided to legalize ADUs citywide.[6]

The construction of ADUs can make an impact in alleviating the housing shortage in California because there are many potential sites where ADUs can be built. For example, under the ADU ordinance in the City of Sunnyvale that was in effect in 2019, 63% of the single-family properties in Sunnyvale could have an ADU.[7] With the passage of the new California ADU laws that will go into effect in 2020, this percentage will likely rise significantly. In addition, the new laws make it possible to construct additional ADUs:

- Two in-law units can be built on a single-family property (See Chapter 2).
- ADUs can be built in areas zoned for multi-family and mixed use.

Benefits to Owners of Homes with ADUs

Building an ADU in California is a win-win situation. It not only helps with the housing shortage in the state; it also brings many benefits to the homeowner. By creating an ADU, a homeowner can take advantage of the following benefits:

- A Way to Take Care of Family

Many middle-aged people face a difficult situation regarding one of their parents' living situation. As the elderly parents get older, they require more assistance, and many do not want to live in senior housing or in an assisted living situation. Some elderly parents may even have the expectation that they will live with their children. However, middle-aged people often have some reservations about parents or in-laws sharing living space in the same house.

In many cases, ADUs provide a great solution to these kinds of situations. With an ADU, family members can be "close but not too close." Senior parents are close enough to provide the necessary assistance and to have time together. Yet, the ADU provides some boundaries which allows for privacy. The boundaries provided by ADUs may also be helpful in cases in which middle-aged people want to provide housing for their children who are in their young adult years. It has become more common for young adults to live in their parents' home. The Pew Research Center reported that in 2014, for the first time in the modern era, the most common living situation for 18 to 34-year-old young adults was living with parents.[8]

- A Source of Extra Income

For people who do not need to provide housing for family members, an ADU can be a significant source of rental income. In October 2019, the average rent for a one-bedroom apartment in Los Angeles and San Francisco was $2499 and $3601, respectively.[9] In addition to generating some income, an ADU can be used for altruistic purposes. Some people may desire to help lower-income people such as students, teachers, and church employees by offering them ADU rentals at a discounted price.

Prior to 2020, some cities in California required that the homeowner reside on the property, in either the main residence or the ADU. This limited the income potential of the property. The new 2020 ADU laws allow homeowners to generate rental income from the main house and one or two ADUs. ADUs that are permitted from January 1, 2020 to December 31, 2024 are exempt from the owner-occupant restriction.

With the current popularity of Airbnb, some people may desire to use Airbnb to generate income through short-term rentals of their ADU. However, the new laws require that the length of an ADU rental be at least 30 days.

- Increased Home Value

In 2013, the National Association of Realtors released a study that showed that in-laws units increased the value of a home. The study found that the rooms in a house that are the most desired are basements and in-law suites. 20 percent of buyers would be willing to pay a median of $2920 more for a house with an in-law unit.[10] Surely, this dollar amount would be greater if the study just accounted for homes in California. Also, *The Wall Street Journal* published an article titled "The Hottest Home Amenity: In-Law Apartments" which pointed out that in the Northern California real estate market, properties with ADUs attract a lot of interest from Asian buyers because of their interest in housing that can accommodate multiple generations.[11]

Difficulties Involved with Building an ADU

Although there are great benefits to having an ADU, it is wise to consider the costs and potential difficulties of building an in-law unit before proceeding with a project.

- Financial Cost

Building an ADU requires a significant financial investment. The simplest and least expensive type of in-law construction is converting part of the living area of an existing house into an ADU. For our project that was completed in 2017, it cost about $86,000 to renovate the back part of our home's first floor into an in-law unit with 497 square feet. In addition, we spent about $14,000 on landscaping to create a patio and to replace the concrete path that leads to the entrance of the in-law unit.

If the project involves new construction, the cost is likely to be higher. At an ADU seminar in May 2019 sponsored by the Housing Trust Silicon Valley, it was estimated that the total cost of a 500 square foot detached ADU would be $268,000.[12] The main costs associated with building an ADU are:

- ☐ Professional fees (architect, structural engineer)
- ☐ City permit fees
- ☐ Impact fees
- ☐ Construction insurance
- ☐ Contractor fees
  - o Demolition
  - o Foundation
  - o Framing and carpentry
  - o Roofing
  - o Plumbing
  - o Electrical upgrade/wiring and gas lines
  - o Heating and air conditioning
  - o Doors and windows
- ☐ Repair of problems found during demolition
- ☐ Utility hookup fees (water, sewage)
- ☐ Finishes (flooring, cabinets, appliances, countertops, lighting, etc.)
- ☐ Parking spaces
- ☐ Landscaping

It is highly recommended that homeowners create a budget before they start building an ADU. In Chapter 7, I provide some details about how our money was spent and a template that you can use to determine a budget.

- Financing

Homeowners typically have limited options when looking for financing for an ADU project. In 2017, UC Berkeley's Terner Center for Housing Innovation did a study of ADUs built in Portland, Seattle and Vancouver, three cities that are considered leaders in ADU construction. This study of 414 ADUs showed that homeowners paid for their ADU in the following manner:[13]

Borrowed against equity in current property	40%
Used personal savings	30%
Used other personal resources	15%
All other	11%
Borrowed against expected future value of ADU	4%

A very small percentage (4%) used a construction loan which allowed the homeowner to borrow against the future value of the ADU.

Major banks typically offer financing that allows a homeowner to borrow against equity in the current property—a home equity line of credit (HELOC) or a cash-out refinance. However, homeowners without a lot of equity in their homes may not be able to get enough money from a HELOC or cash-out refinance to pay for an ADU. Homeowners may be able to find a regional bank or credit union which offers a construction loan for an ADU project. Chapter 7 has more information about obtaining financing for an ADU.

- Time

Be aware! Taking on an ADU construction project requires a lot of time and effort. It is similar to having a part-time job as a project manager. During the project, the homeowner may have to spend time on:

- □ Working with a designer and/or architect. Designing all the details of an ADU can be a time-consuming task.
- □ Working with the contractor and construction workers. As the construction proceeds, the homeowner may have many decisions to make on the details of the project.
- □ Getting permits from the city.
- □ Doing research about different housing finishes (cabinets, countertop, tile, appliances, etc.) and purchasing items.

Homeowners can save money on finishes if they spend the time to find good quality products at discounted prices. In Chapter 7, I will give some suggestions about how you can save money on finishes.

- Legal Requirements

Prior to 2017, there were many barriers to building an in-law unit in California. Some of the barriers to building an ADU included:

- □ **Prohibitions against ADUs.** For example, the city of Newport Beach prohibited ADUs entirely.
- □ **Parking Space Requirements.** Cities often required homeowners to make provisions for new parking spaces for vehicles.
- □ **Fire Safety Requirements.** California Residential Code section

R313.2 requires the installation of automatic residential fire sprinkler systems in newly constructed buildings. Some ADU projects were required to have a sprinkler system, and others were required to have a fire wall between the main residence and ADU.

- **Utility Connection Fees.** A person who constructed an ADU near Santa Cruz was forced to pay over $20,000 in water hookup fees.[14]
- **Permitting Process and Fees.** A Menlo Park resident who converted a garage into an in-law unit paid about $15,000 in permit fees and endured a difficult permit process.[15]
- **Impact Fees.** Some cities required homeowners who want to build an ADU to pay large fees for community services (e.g. parks, schools). In August 2019, the Terner Center released a report that showed that the impact fees for a single-family home in Los Angeles and Oakland are $10,933 and $28,000, respectively.[16]
- **Homeowner Associations.** Some homeowner's associations placed restrictions on the construction of ADUs.

Fortunately, the 2017 and 2020 ADU laws have made building an in-law unit much easier. Local governments and homeowner's associations are no longer allowed to prohibit ADUs. In addition, the bills have reduced the barriers in the other five areas mentioned above – parking space requirements, fire safety requirements, utility connection fees, permitting process and fees, and impact fees. In the next chapter of this book, the ramifications of new laws will be highlighted, as they may influence your decision about how you build an ADU.

After the state of California passed the 2017 ADU laws, many cities revised or created an ordinance to comply with the new laws. By May 2019, about 200 of the 482 cities in California had passed an ADU ordinance that complied with the 2017 laws.[17] In 2020, these cities will have to update their ADU ordinances to comply with the new 2020 laws. All local ordinances must be as permissive as the state ADU laws. However, the state allows local governments some freedom to determine local ADU regulations. For a specific ADU regulation, the local ordinance may be more permissive than the state law. Therefore, each local ordinance is unique, and it is important for homeowners to study and understand the local ADU ordinance for their city or county.

The 2017 ADU laws encouraged many more people to apply for an ADU permit. From 2016 to 2017, the number of building permits for ADUs in California increased 63 percent.[18] In particular, the City of Los Angeles has seen a huge growth in the number of ADU permits. In 2016, Los Angeles issued 117 ADU permits. In 2018, the number of ADU permits issued by the city had grown to 4,155.[19] Although every city is not experiencing this type of explosive growth, the new 2020 laws likely will spur continued growth in the construction of ADUs.

There is another source that could create more ADUs in California. In the past, many people added an unpermitted in-law unit to their property and illegally rented out the unit. One of the new 2020 ADU laws, SB 13, creates an amnesty program for homeowners who have an unpermitted, substandard ADU:

> This bill grants an ADU owner with a non-compliant ADU a delay to make the necessary changes to bring the ADU up to code. The delay applies to changes that, in the judgment of the local building official, and in consultation with fire and

code enforcement officers, is not necessary to protect the health and safety of the building residents.[20]

This amnesty program is in effect until January 1, 2025.

The new 2020 ADU laws have removed a lot of local regulations that hindered the construction of ADUs. Although homeowners still face challenges in building an ADU, the new laws clearly make it easier. Once homeowners decide that they want to start an ADU project, one of the first steps is deciding what type of ADU to build.

(Chapter 1 Endnotes)

[1] Elijah Chiland, "LA Home Prices Inch up to an All-Time High," *Curbed Los Angeles, July 26, 2019. https://la.curbed.com/2019/7/26/8931996/los-angeles-median-home-price-record-high.*

[2] Zillow.com. "Fremont Home Prices & Values," https://www.zillow.com/fremont-ca/home-values. Accessed November 7, 2019.

[3] Orange County Register Editorial Board, "Rising Rents a Symptom of California's Housing Crisis," *Orange County Register, October 17, 2017. https://www.ocregister.com/2017/10/17/rising-rents-a-symptom-of-californias-housing-crisis/*

[4] California Department of Housing and Community Development, "Accessory Dwelling Unit Memorandum," December 2018. https://www.hcd.ca.gov/policy-research/docs/ADU-TA-Memorandum.pdf, 2.

[5] Michael Litchfield, In-Laws, Outlaws, and Granny Flats (Newtown, CT: The Taunton Press, 2011), 10.

[6] David Garcia, "ADU Update: Early Lessons and Impacts of California's State and Local Policy Changes," Terner Center for Housing Innovation, UC Berkeley, December 21, 2017. https://ternercenter.berkeley.edu/blog/adu-update-early-lessons-and-impacts-of-californias-state-and-local-policy.

[7] Shila Behzadiari (2019, May 17). ADUs: Not Just for Granny Anymore, Seminar sponsored by AARP and Housing Trust Silicon Valley, San Jose, CA.

[8] Richard Fry, "For First Time in Modern Era, Living with Parents Edges Out Other Living Arrangements for 18- to 34-Year-Olds," Pew Research Center, May 24, 2016. www.pewsocialtrends.org/2016/05/24/for-first-time-in-modern-era-living-with-parents-edges-out-other-living-arrangements-for-18-to-34-year-olds/

[9] Rent Jungle, "Rent Trend Data in Los Angeles, California." https://www.rentjungle.com/average-rent-in-los-angeles-rent-trends/. "Rent Trend Data in San Francisco, California." https://www.rentjungle.com/average-rent-in-san-francisco-rent-trends/. Accessed November 9, 2019

[10] National Association of Realtors, "Buyers Value Storage Space, In-Law Suites, NAR Survey Finds," March 13, 2013. https://www.nar.realtor/newsroom/buyers-value-storage-space-in-law-suites-nar-survey-finds.

[11] Katy McLaughlin, "The Hottest Home Amenity: In-Law Apartments," The Wall Street Journal, November 6, 2014. https://www.wsj.com/articles/the-hottest-home-amenity-in-law-apartments-1415288579.

[12] Steve Vallejos (2019, May 4), Small Homes, Big Impact: South County ADU Workshop, Sponsored by Housing Trust Silicon Valley, Morgan Hill, CA.

[13] Karen Chapple, Jake Wegmann, Farzad Mashhood and Rebecca Coleman, Jumpstarting the Market for Accessory Dwelling Units: Lessons Learned from Portland, Seattle and Vancouver, Terner Center for Housing Innovation, UC Berkeley, April 2017, 20.

[14] Kathleen Pender, "New California Housing Laws Make Granny Units Easier to Build," *San Francisco Chronicle, December 3, 2016. https://www.sfchronicle.com/news/article/New-California-housing-laws-make-granny-units-10688483.php.*

[15] Alana Semuels, "Little Homes in Big Backyards: San Francisco's Housing Solution?" *The Atlantic, February 18, 2016. https://www.theatlantic.com/business/archive/2016/02/little-homes-in-big-backyards-san-franciscos-housing-solution/463326/.*

[16] Terner Center for Housing Innovation, UC Berkeley, Residential Impact Fees in California, August 5, 2019, p. 45

[17] Bob Wieckowski, (2019, May 17), ADUs: Not Just for Granny Anymore, Seminar sponsored by AARP and Housing Trust Silicon Valley, San Jose, CA.

[18] Daren Blomquist, "The Promise and Pitfalls of ADUs as Affordable Housing Panacea," Attom Data Solutions, April 6, 2018. https://www.attomdata.com/news/affordability/promise-pitfalls-adus-affordable-housing-panacea/

[19] Los Angeles City Planning Department Quarterly Newsletter, Summer 2019, 11. https://planning.lacity.org/odocument/c677b589-a30e-4fb9-a614-000c39e308ab/2019_SUMMER.pdf

[20] California Legislative Information, SB-13 Accessory Dwelling Units: 09/13/19 – Senate Floor Analyses, https://leginfo.legislature.ca.gov/faces/billAnalysisClient.xhtml?bill_id=201920200SB13

My mother had specifically said that she wanted to live in an in-law unit but didn't want to be in a separate building. Therefore, as we looked for a property to buy, one of our main concerns was how we would create an in-law unit that would be attached to the main house.

Other people may prefer to build an ADU that is detached from the main house in order to give themselves more privacy. In this chapter, we will look at several different types of ADUs, some attached and others detached, that a homeowner may choose to build:

- New detached building (cottage)
- Extension from the main house
- Garage conversion - attached or detached
- Conversion of existing living space (JADU – junior accessory dwelling unit)

Homeowners may also consider the possibility of building two ADUs. One of the new 2020 California ADU laws, Assembly Bill 68, makes it possible to build two ADUs on a single-family lot—one JADU (attached) and one ADU (detached).

There are a few other less common types of ADUs that are not covered in detail in this chapter:

- Conversion of a basement. For this type of ADU, an external entrance for the ADU must be constructed.

- Conversion of an attic. For this type of ADU, an external staircase to access the ADU must be constructed.

- ADU on top of a detached garage. This type of ADU, which is typically expensive to build, requires a structurally sound garage that can support a second story. An external staircase to access the ADU must be constructed.

Before a homeowner can decide which type of in-law unit to build, it is necessary to understand how California's ADU laws apply to each different type of ADU. The following section provides an analysis of the different types of ADUs and the effect of the ADU laws on each type of ADU. Then, you can decide which type will be feasible on your property and will best meet your needs.

Before analyzing the different types of ADUs, it is important to understand one basic term about properties—setbacks. Cities typically have specifications about how close dwellings can be to the homeowner's property lines. These specifications vary depending on the zoning of a homeowner's property. At the time that we built our ADU, the City of Fremont's setback requirements for our house were 20 feet in the front of the house, 25 feet in the back of the house, and 6 feet on the side of the house. The state of California's 2020 ADU laws have reduced setbacks in the backyard and side yard, making it much easier to build an ADU.

New Construction: Cottage or Extension from Main House

The 2020 California ADU laws have made it much easier for a homeowner to add a detached ADU or extension ADU in the backyard or side yard of their property. However, in some locations, these types of ADUs cannot be built. For example, in most locations in San Francisco, it is not possible to build a detached or extension ADU because the houses are tightly bunched together and have no side yard. An ADU must have its own entrance and a pathway to the entrance. Most homes in San Francisco do not have space for a pathway.

The ideal situation for a detached or extension ADU is when the homeowner has a large backyard or side yard and can create a pathway to the entrance. The following section has information about the pros and cons of a cottage and extension ADU.

New Detached Building (Cottage)

Many people favor a detached cottage because it provides some separation and privacy from the main dwelling unit. This is particularly important if the ADU is going to be used as a rental unit.

- Potential Issues

  - **Cost.** The cost of building a cottage is typically moderate to high because a new foundation will have to be built and utility lines will have to be run to the cottage. However, homeowners have the option of purchasing a prefabricated (modular) or manufactured ADU model that can lower their cost. As the popularity of ADUs in California has grown, some companies have designed ADU models that can be built in a factory and then placed on a homeowner's property. Chapter 5 has more information about purchasing a prefabricated or manufactured ADU.

☐ **Distance requirement from the main house.** The state law does not specify the minimum distance between the main house and the ADU. Each city's ordinance sets the minimum distance, which is typically six to ten feet.

Extension from the Main House

A homeowner may create an ADU by building an extension or "bump out" from the main house. Although an extension ADU has less privacy than a cottage, it has some advantages. Since the ADU is close to the existing house, it is easier to tap into the existing utility lines.

- Potential Issues

    ☐ **Difficult to blend the ADU with the existing house.** Ideally, the extension will blend in well with the existing house. Michael Litchfield, author of *In-laws, Outlaws and Granny Flats*, points out that adding a bump-out may make the house look too big and block light.[1] Architectural skill will be required to make the resulting house function well and look aesthetically pleasing.

    ☐ **The wall between the main house and ADU may require a seismic upgrade.** If changes are made to the wall between the main house and ADU (e.g. doors or windows added or removed), then the city may require that the wall be seismically upgraded. This could cost thousands of dollars.

Impact of the New Laws on Cottages and Extensions

- **Reduced setback requirements.** The 2020 California ADU law states that the setback requirement for the backyard and side yard cannot be more than four feet. This opens up the possibility for many homeowners to build a cottage or extension ADU.

- **Prohibit local building laws from restricting a "standard ADU."** Local governments must allow an ADU with the following characteristics (which I call a "standard ADU"):

  ☐ Size equal to or less than 800 square feet
  ☐ Height at least 16 feet tall
  ☐ Setbacks of four feet for the side and rear yards
  Prior to 2020, local governments could restrict the construction of ADUs by using the following rules:
  ☐ Minimum or maximum size of ADU
  ☐ Size based upon a percentage of the primary dwelling
  ☐ Lot coverage
  ☐ Floor area ratio
  ☐ Open space
  ☐ Minimum lot size
  Now, local governments cannot use the above rules to prohibit a "standard ADU."

- **Prohibition of restrictive maximum square footage rules.** Local governments cannot set a maximum square footage rule for an ADU:

  ☐ Less than 850 square feet for a one-bedroom ADU.

  ☐ Less than 1000 square feet for an ADU with more than one bedroom.

  However, homeowners must still comply with the State of California's law for the maximum size of an ADU.

  ☐ An attached ADU shall not exceed 50 percent of the existing living area.

  ☐ A detached ADU shall not exceed 1,200 square feet.

- **Reduced parking space requirements.** The parking space requirement shall not exceed:

  ☐ One parking space for a studio or one-bedroom ADU

  ☐ Two parking spaces for a two-bedroom ADU

  The parking space may be tandem (one car behind another in a driveway) or in a setback area as long as the local government does not find any hazardous conditions (e.g. fire). Also, there is no parking space requirement if the location of the property meets any of the following conditions:

  ☐ Within one-half mile walking distance of public transit.

  ☐ In an architecturally and historically significant district.

  ☐ In an area where on-street parking permits are required but are not offered to the ADU occupant.

  ☐ Within one block of a car share area.

  Cities may choose to waive the parking space requirement.

- **No special fire safety requirements.** The new 2020 ADU law states, "Accessory dwelling units shall not be required to provide fire sprinklers if they are not required for the main residence."[2]

- **More reasonable utility connection fees.** A local utility may require an additional connection between the ADU and the utility. However, the connection fee or capacity charge must be proportionate to the burden of the ADU based on either its square footage or the number of plumbing fixtures.

- **Reduced impact fees.** The new 2020 ADU law states, "A local agency, special district, or water corporation shall not impose any impact fee upon the development of an accessory dwelling unit less than 750 square feet. Any impact fees charged for an accessory dwelling unit of 750 square feet or more shall be charged proportionately in relation to the square footage of the primary dwelling unit."[3]

Summary – Building a Cottage or Extension ADU

The 2020 California ADU laws are very favorable to homeowners provided that their ADU is not too big. In general, I recommend that a homeowner builds a "standard ADU" of less than 750 square feet with four-foot setbacks. Local building laws and codes cannot prevent a homeowner from building an ADU like this. If a homeowner builds an ADU of 750 square feet or greater, then impact fees may be assessed. If the size is greater than 800 square feet, then the local government's building laws and codes may hinder the ADU project.

Garage Conversion

Many people think that converting a garage is a good way to create an ADU. Whether the garage is attached or detached, this strategy does not require the construction of a new structure. In San Francisco, since it is not feasible for most homeowners to build a cottage or extension ADU due to the lack of a side yard, it has become popular to convert existing garage space to an ADU. A typical San Francisco house has a large garage on the first floor and one or more stories of living space above the garage. San Francisco homeowners can use part of the garage space to build an ADU and create an entrance to the ADU at the front of the garage.

However, in many cases, ADU expert Kol Peterson has found that garage conversions are not prudent. He writes, "Half of my ADU consultations are spent on reviewing options for garage conversions and informing clients about shortcomings of a garage conversion. This often pops the dreams of a conversion." Peterson has found that many older garages are not structurally sound and would require a large amount of money to have them comply with building codes.[4]

- Ideal Situation

  Converting an existing garage is a good solution when:
  - ☐ The garage is in good condition and can be brought up to current building code standards at a reasonable cost.

- Potential Issues

  - □ **Condition of the garage.** Before a homeowner pursues a garage conversion, it is necessary to have a structural engineer evaluate the condition of the garage.
  - □ **Size limitations.** A small one-car garage can only be converted into a studio. A smaller two-car garage (20 feet x 20 feet) provides only 400 square feet of space.

- Impact of the New Laws

  - □ **No setback requirement.** There are no setback requirements for an existing garage that is converted to an ADU.
  - □ **No replacement parking required.** The new 2020 ADU law states, "When a garage, carport or covered parking structure is demolished in conjunction with the construction of an accessory dwelling unit or converted to an accessory dwelling unit, the local agency shall not require that those off-street parking spaces be replaced."[5]
  - □ **No utility connection and capacity fees.** Local utility companies are not allowed to charge connection and capacity fees for ADUs that are contained within an existing residence or accessory structure.
  - □ **No special fire safety requirements.** ADUs are not required to have fire sprinklers if they are not required for the main residence.
  - □ **Typically no impact fees.** Impact fees can only be assessed on ADU that are 750 square feet or larger. ADUs created by a garage conversion are usually less than 750 square feet.

☐ **Limited expansion allowed when converting a detached garage.** The new 2020 ADU laws allow a homeowner to extend a detached garage by up to 150 square feet to accommodate entering and exiting the ADU.

Conversion of Existing Living Space

If a homeowner converts part of their house into an in-law unit, they will be creating a special type of ADU called a Junior Accessory Dwelling Unit (JADU). A JADU is usually less costly and easier to build because the existing footprint of the home is not changed, which makes the construction of the JADU less complex.

- Ideal Situation

Building a JADU is a good solution when the homeowner has a part of their home that can be sectioned off to create a separate unit. Perhaps the homeowner has extra room in their house because their children have moved out. In carving out part of their home to create a JADU, the homeowner must create a separate outside entrance for the JADU, and an entrance into the JADU from the main home. There are two types of houses that are ideal for building a JADU:
  - A one-story ranch-style home in which one side or the back of the house can be converted into an in-law unit.
  - A two-story house in which part of the first floor can be converted into an in-law unit.

- Potential Issues

  - **Size Limitation.** The State of California's law limits the size of a JADU to a maximum of 500 square feet.
  - **Appropriate Space.** The homeowner needs to consider this question: "Within the existing footprint of the house, is there

a space that the I can convert into a JADU?" Keep in mind that the law requires that the converted space includes an existing bedroom.

☐ **The external walls of the JADU may require a seismic upgrade.** If changes are made to the external walls of the JADU (e.g. doors or windows added or removed), then the city may require that the wall be seismically upgraded. We had to spend more than $6000 to strengthen the walls of our JADU.

- Impact of the New Laws

  ☐ **A second kitchen is allowed.** Prior to the passage of the ADU laws, local regulations typically did not allow homeowners to have more than one kitchen in a single-family residence. A big benefit of the new ADU laws is that they allow for an additional kitchen in an attached in-law unit. The law actually requires that a JADU have an efficiency kitchen.

  ☐ **No bathroom required.** A separate bathroom for a JADU is optional. The JADU may share a bathroom with the main dwelling.

  ☐ **No parking space requirement.** The homeowner is not required to build additional parking spaces.

  ☐ **No special fire safety requirements.** A JADU is not considered a new or separate unit for fire safety purposes.

  ☐ **No utility connection and capacity fees.** A JADU is not considered to be a new or separate unit when determining utility connection and capacity fees. We were pleased that our local sanitary district informed us that we would not be subject to its one-time capacity charge of $6211 because we were converting existing space. However, we were charged an annual sewer service fee of $341 because our house is now considered to be a multi-family residential dwelling unit.

☐ **No impact fees.** There are no impact fees for JADUs.

Adding Two ADUs to a Single-Family Lot

Homeowners who want to maximize rental income or create two ADUs for family members can take advantage of the new 2020 ADU law that allows one attached JADU and one detached ADU on a single-family lot. The detached unit may be built by one of following two methods:

☐ Convert an existing accessory structure, such as a garage. Homeowners can add 150 square feet to the accessory structure to accommodate entering and exiting the ADU.

☐ Construct a new detached cottage with four-foot setbacks. Local government can limit the ADU to 800 square feet and the height of the unit to 16 feet.

For more information on JADUs, garage conversions and detached cottages, see the sections earlier in this chapter.

Multi-Family Dwelling Structures

Owners of a multi-family dwelling structure (duplex, triplex, fourplex, apartment building, condominiums, townhouses) can add ADUs to their properties. There are two possible ways to build ADUs:

- ☐ **Conversion of existing space.** Owners can add at least one ADU within an existing multifamily dwelling by using unused space (e.g. storage rooms, boiler rooms, passageways, attics, basements or garages). Each ADU must comply with state building standards for dwellings.
- ☐ **New construction.** Two detached ADUs may be added to the lot that already has a multifamily dwelling structure. The ADUs are subject to a height limitation of 16 and setbacks of four feet in the backyard and side yard.

Special Circumstance: Conversion and Expansion

Creating an in-law unit was only part of our remodeling strategy. Our house originally had 1722 square feet, of which 497 square feet went to the junior accessory dwelling unit. We felt that the remaining square footage was not enough for our needs. Therefore, we wanted to extend the first floor so there could be a larger piano studio with a small restroom. We also wanted to extend the second floor to create more living space on the second floor. As a result, our project had two phases – the first phase was creating the in-law unit, and the second phase was extending the house and renovating the second floor.

If you want to do this type of project, then it is very important to plan ahead and to thoroughly understand the local laws. We ran into a big problem with our project because we didn't know about a particular local law. The next chapter focuses on some local laws that affect the construction of in-law units. Before you can finalize your plans about what type of in-law unit you want to build, it is important to make sure that your plans comply with the local laws.

(Chapter 2 Endnotes)

[1] Michael Litchfield, *In-Laws, Outlaws, and Granny Flats (Newtown, CT: The Taunton Press, 2011),* 32.

[2] Section 65852.2 of Government Code, subsection (a) (1) (D) (xii)

[3] Section 65852.2 of Government Code, subsection (f) (3)

[4] Kol Peterson, *Backdoor Revolution: The Definitive Guide to ADU Development (Portland: Accessory Dwelling Strategies, LLC, 2018),* 58.

[5] Section 65852.2 of Government Code, subsection (a) (1) (D) (xi)

While the in-law unit was under construction at the back of the house, we began to plan an extension at the front of our house. Both the first and second floors would be pushed out, which would provide more room for my wife's piano studio and our living space. Part of the second-floor extension would be built on top of our existing garage, so we would add more square footage on the second floor (about 300 square feet) than the first floor (about 100 square feet). After the planned extension was completed, we figured that there would be about 1280 square feet of living space on the second floor. We were excited about having the extra square footage on the second floor and spent a lot of time designing the new layout of our house.

When I went to the City of Fremont to discuss our extension plan, I found out about a particular city rule that had a huge impact on us. This "floor area ratio" rule limits the amount of square footage on the second floor of a house in order to protect the privacy of neighboring residences. The ratio of the square footage on the second floor to the square footage on the first floor (living space plus garage) cannot exceed 60%. The ratio for our house, which was about 85%, already exceeded the allowable ratio by a large amount. We tried to figure out a way to enlarge the first floor in order to decrease the ratio. This would allow us to add more square footage on the second floor, but unfortunately, it was not possible.

The only way to get around this rule was to go through the process of having a public hearing. However, we decided that it was not worth the time and money to do this. As a result of this rule, we were not able to build an extension to the second floor. That was disappointing and frustrating! We had to alter our plans and make do with a smaller second floor. Our altered plans will be described later in the book in Chapter 8.

Local ADU Ordinances

Although the new 2020 ADU laws severely limit local government's restrictions on the construction of ADUs, homeowners should still research their local government's ADU ordinance. If a local government has not passed an ADU ordinance, then the state of California's ADU laws are in effect in that jurisdiction. Here are two important rules that may be found in local ADU ordinances:

- Prohibitions in Certain Areas or Zones

Some local governments have passed laws that prevent ADUs from being constructed in certain locations. For example, the County of Los Angeles passed an ordinance that prohibits the construction of ADUs in some specific areas. The county does not allow the construction of ADUs in areas that are designated as "Very High Fire Hazard Severity Zones."[1]

- Owner-occupancy

Prior to the new 2020 ADU laws, some cities required that homeowners either live in the main residence or the ADU. The new 2020 ADU laws override the owner-occupancy rule of local ordinances for five years. ADUs that are permitted from January 1, 2020 to December 31, 2024 are exempt from the owner-occupant restriction.

□ Homeowners who live in a city that does not have an owner-occupancy restriction can rent the main residence and one or two ADUs.

□ For homeowner who live in a city that has an owner-occupancy restriction:

  o If the ADU was permitted before 2020, the owner must live in either the main residence or ADU.

  o If the ADU is permitted from 2020 to 2024, the owner does not have to live in the main residence or ADU.

There is some uncertainty about the effect of the new 2020 owner-occupancy law on JADUs. Prior to 2020, the state had passed a JADU law that required homeowners to live in either the main house or JADU. Does the new 2020 owner-occupancy law take precedence over the prior JADU law? My belief is that the new 2020 law takes precedence, and that the owner-occupancy requirement for JADUs is suspended for five years. However, I saw a city's website that stated that owner-occupancy is still required for JADUs.

Two Cases in which Local Laws Have a Big Impact

- **When building an ADU that is larger than 800 square feet**

Local ordinances cannot prohibit a "standard ADU" of 800 square feet or less (See Chapter 2). However, if a proposed ADU is larger than 800 square feet, local rules can hinder the construction of the ADU. These rules may include the maximum size of an ADU and lot coverage.

For an ADU greater than 800 square feet, a local government may set the maximum ADU size based on the size of the lot. For example, here are the City of Fremont's lot size requirements for larger ADUs:[2]

Lot Size (sq. ft.)	ADU Maximum Size (sq. ft.)
10,000-19,999	900
20,000-39,999	1,050
40,000 or more	1,200

A homeowner in Fremont would need to have a very large lot in order to build an ADU larger than 800 square feet.

Also, lot coverage can also limit the size of an ADU. Local governments typically have a rule about how much of a homeowner's property can have buildings on it. This is done by setting the maximum percentage of the land that can have buildings. Typically, this percentage is 30% to 40%.[3] For example, if the size of the homeowner's lot is 6000 square feet and the local government's maximum lot coverage percentage is 40%, then the homeowner can only have buildings on 2400 square feet of the property. If the main dwelling unit's living space and garage cover 1600 square feet, then the size of a new attached or detached ADU can only be 800 square feet.

- **When building an ADU and doing an extension of the main house.**

If a project involves an extension of the main house along with the construction of an ADU, the homeowner should be aware that the favorable state ADU laws apply only to the construction of the ADU, not to the extension of the main house. The homeowner must comply with the local building rules, such as lot coverage and floor area ratio, when planning the extension of the main house. The introduction to this chapter illustrated how the "floor area ratio" rule could hinder an extension project.

This chapter does not provide an exhaustive list of all the different local laws that may affect an ADU project. It is very important for a homeowner who wants to build an ADU to research the local housing laws. Often, a homeowner can find the information on the Internet. In addition, it may be helpful to speak with an architect who has done work in the city or area which will issue the building permit. The architect probably will be aware of issues that could cause problems with an ADU project. This can save the homeowner a lot of time and trouble!

(Chapter 3 Endnotes)

[1] Los Angeles County Department of Regional Planning, "An Ordinance Amending Title 22 (Planning and Zoning) of the Los Angeles County Code Related to Accessory Dwelling Units," http://planning.lacounty.gov/assets/upl/case/ 2017-004091_attachmentC-20180124.pdf. Accessed March 12, 2018, 12.

[2] City of Fremont Community Development Department, "Accessory Dwelling Units," April 2017. https://fremont.gov/DocumentCenter/Home/View/4073.

[3] Litchfield, *In-Laws, Outlaws, and Granny Flats*, 12.

We had completed our plans for the in-law unit and were eager to get started on the construction. After submitting our plans to the City of Fremont on June 13, 2017, we expected to receive a building permit within three weeks, which was the normal time for the city to process the application. Unfortunately, we started to hear about problems from our contractor, who was actively trying to get our application through the permitting process. The City of Fremont told him that the size of our in-law unit exceeded the maximum size for a junior accessory dwelling unit (500 square feet). This was rather strange because on our plan, the in-law unit had a size of 497 square feet. The city believed that the width of the in-law unit was 45 feet, rather than 37 feet 9 inches, which was shown on our plan. Our contractor tried to convince the city officials that the in-law unit was not that wide, but they had some documentation that showed that it was 45 feet wide. In addition, the city communicated that it had no record that the main residence's kitchen was built upstairs. The city wanted some proof that the house was permitted with the kitchen on the second floor. We were almost certain that the kitchen had been built on the second floor during the original construction of the house, but we had no proof. The processing of the permit application was stalled, and we didn't know what to do.

Eight weeks after we submitted the application, we received a letter from the City of Fremont, which was written by an employee who had the title of "Plans Examiner". The letter stated the city's position on our permit application:

> The existing first and second floor plans as shown on the project submittal package do not match city records. Please clarify. If city records are incorrect, please provide previously approved plans showing that there were bedrooms on the first floor and the kitchen was permitted to be on the second floor. If unpermitted, please legalize work as part of this permit. Provide plans and details to legalize all unpermitted work if applicable.

The examiner also included drawings of the floor layout that the city had on file. When I looked at the drawings, it was clear that the layout was not for our house. For some reason, the City of Fremont had the wrong drawings on file for our house. Therefore, I decided to go to the city offices to do some detective work. I found the permit history for our house, including the original permit that was issued in 1962. Unfortunately, the original permit did not contain detailed drawings of the floor layout. I asked a city employee if I could look at the drawings for our house, but she told me that it would take a while to get access. Therefore, I decided that the best thing to do was to set up a meeting with the examiner who had sent us the letter. I made a copy of the original permit, which showed that the width of the in-law unit was not 45 feet. Also, I noticed that on the original permit, there was a note that stated, "Plan 24 in lieu of 29." I thought that this might be the issue that was causing the problems. I suspected that our residence was part of a development that had multiple house plans. It appeared to me that there had been a change of plans for our lot, and that the city had not recorded this change.

Our contractor came along with me to the meeting with the examiner. During the meeting, the examiner told us that we could look at the drawings for our house on microfiche. I couldn't remember the last time I had used microfiche! The examiner gave us the microfiche for Plan 24, and we went to use the microfiche machine. When we looked at the Plan 24 drawings, it was clear it did not have the correct layout for our house. Then, I asked the examiner for the drawings for Plan 29. It turned out that this was the correct plan for our house. The back of the house, where our in-law unit would be located, was 37 feet 10 inches wide (only one inch different from our measurement). As we looked at the plan's second floor, we noticed that it had a large unfinished area where our kitchen is located. Clearly, the original owner of our house decided to build the kitchen in the unfinished area on the second floor. The mystery was solved! We informed the city examiner that Plan 29 had the correct drawings for our house. A short time later, we were issued a permit to build the in-law unit.

Permit History

The moral of the story is that a homeowner who wants to build an ADU should make a visit to their local government's office and do thorough research about their house. Even if a homeowner has lived in their house for many years and knows a lot about their house's history, I would still recommend this. It is especially important if a person is in the process of purchasing a new property and plans to construct an ADU. A good time to do this research is during the contingency period of a home sale, when a buyer typically reviews the seller's disclosure package and arranges home inspections. Before removing the inspection contingency, the buyer should find out about the property's permit history. The buyer may uncover information that would affect an ADU project. For example, the buyer may find out that the house has an open permit or that certain work on the house was not permitted.

Our house used to have a pool in the backyard, but the previous owner decided to fill it with dirt. The previous owner received a permit to fill in the pool, but we found out that a permit was not issued for the dirt compaction in the pool. As a result, if we wanted to build something on top of the pool, we would first have to remove the dirt in the pool and then have it compacted according to code. Our contractor told us that this would cost a lot of money. As a result, we decided not to do any new construction in our backyard.

Public Utility Easements and Power Lines

It is important for homeowners to find out if there is a public utility easement on their property. If there is a power pole or power lines on or near the property, then the local electric utility company may have an easement on the homeowner's property. An easement gives the local utility the right to access the homeowner's property for installations and maintenance. In addition, the local utility has the right to determine what can be built in the easement area. This can be a hinderance to homeowners who want to build an ADU.

In Los Angeles, hundreds of ADU projects have been stalled or blocked due to a power line easement.[1] Los Angeles homeowners who want to build an ADU need to be aware of the following requirements for power lines and easements:

- The California Public Utilities Commission General Order 95 Requirement does not allow the construction of new buildings within 6 feet of primary electrical wires.[2] This means that an ADU must be located at least 6 feet away from a main power line. Some homeowners desire to convert a detached garage that is located close to the edge of their properties, where the power lines are located. The Los Angeles Department of Water & Power (LADWP) has stalled or blocked many projects like this due to the proximity of the garage to power lines.
- The LADWP generally has a 5-foot easement from power lines.[3] If the homeowner is building an ADU within 10 feet of an easement line, then the LADWP requires that the homeowner apply for an encroachment clearance.

In the last three chapters, we have examined how different factors influence the planning of an ADU. It may seem like there is a lot of research to do before building an in-law unit—ADU laws, local housing laws, and the house's history. However, making the investment of time in doing this research may save the homeowner a lot of time, money, and headaches. So, I encourage you to put on your detective hat and do the research!

(Chapter 4 Endnotes)

[1] Elijah Chilland, "Power Lines Preventing LA Homeowners from Building ADUs," Curbed Los Angeles, November 27, 2018. https://la.curbed.com/2018/11/27/18069692/los-angeles-adu-construction-granny-flats-dwp

[2] Los Angeles Department of Water & Power, Pole Spotter Flyer. https://www.ladwp.com/ladwp/faces/ladwp/partners/p-constructionservices/p-cs-electricservices/p-cs-es-constructionnearpowerlines?_adf.ctrl-state=pqgxj3f5_834, Accessed December 4, 2019

[3] Los Angeles Department of Water & Power, Pole Spotter Flyer.

After we purchased our house in Fremont, our real estate agent recommended an interior design company which had won a "Best of Houzz Service Award" in 2017. The owner of this company told our real estate agent that in addition to interior design, the company now did architecture. As a result, the company could provide both interior design and architectural services to us. It sounded like a good idea to hire just one company, so after meeting with the owner, we signed a contract with this company to work on our ADU and the extension of the main house. After the interior design company completed the floor plan of the in-law unit, we prepared to submit a permit application to the City of Fremont. However, our contractor told us that the interior design company's drawings were not architectural drawings and thus, were not suitable to get a permit issued. Our contractor tried to show the interior design company how to produce architectural drawings that would be acceptable. The interior design company spent some time trying to create architectural drawings, but it soon became clear that they could not do architecture. What a disappointment! A lot of time was wasted, and we were very upset that the interior design company could not deliver what was promised. We set up a meeting with the owner and asked for a refund for a portion of their fee. The owner understood that we were upset with the time lost and gave us a partial refund.

The success of an in-law unit project is largely dependent on the homeowner hiring the right people for the job. This chapter focuses on helping the homeowner choose the right professionals to work on an ADU project.

The Phases of an ADU Project

Before selecting professionals to work on an ADU project, it is important to understand that a typical project has two different phases:

- Design

In the design phase, the homeowner works with an architect or designer to determine a suitable design for the ADU. The homeowner may also need to hire a structural engineer in certain circumstances, such as when a garage is being converted. After consulting with the homeowner, the architect/designer and structural engineer create drawings for submission to the local government. Then, the contractor or homeowner submits a permit application, which includes the drawings, to the local government. The new 2020 ADU laws require that the local government respond to a permit application within 60 days. The local government may approve the permit application and issue a permit, or respond with a list of comments that need to be addressed by the architect and/or structural engineer.

• Build

Once the homeowner pays the permit fees, the contractor can begin the ADU building project, which typically has three components:

☐ **Demolition and site preparation.** For a JADU or a garage conversion, the contractor will likely have to tear down or remove parts of the existing building (e.g. walls, windows and electrical wiring). For a detached cottage or extension, the contractor will have to prepare the site for the laying of the foundation.

☐ **Building the physical structure.** The contractor lays the new foundation, builds new walls and installs roofing. In addition, the contractor puts in the sheet rock, doors, windows, the electrical system, gas lines, plumbing, and heating, ventilation and air conditioning (HVAC).

☐ **Installing Finishes.** Based on the finishes that the homeowner chooses, the contractor installs cabinets, countertops, tile, flooring, electrical fixtures, and appliances. In addition, the ADU is painted.

The Advantage of Hiring a Single Company

Because of the problem we had with the interior design company, we had to hire an architect to create drawings for the permit application for our ADU. As a result, we ended up working with three different professionals (interior designer, architect and contractor). For our remodeling of the main house, we also needed a structural engineer, so we were working with four different individuals. After the troubles that we encountered trying to coordinate with these different people, I have concluded that if possible, it is preferable to work with a single company on an ADU project. Many ADU companies offer design– build services, which allow the homeowner to interact with only one company. If the homeowner is building a detached cottage, there is an opportunity to further simplify the project by choosing a modular or manufactured ADU.

Modular and Manufactured ADUs

Although a detached cottage tends to be more expensive than other types of ADUs, a homeowner can typically save time and money by choosing a modular (prefab) or manufactured ADU. The following table displays the difference between modular and manufactured ADUs.[1]

Modular (Prefab)	Manufactured
Must conform to local and state building codes	Must meet federal construction standards
Typically built on slab foundation	Typically built on a raised foundation with steel piers
No steel chassis	Transported on a steel chassis that is never removed.

The building timeline for a modular or manufactured ADU tends to be shorter than for an ADU built using conventional construction, which typically takes three months. A modular or manufactured ADU can be built in a factory over a period of two to three weeks.[2] Also, it is possible for certain modular or manufactured ADU designs to be preapproved by a city's building department. This eliminates the need to apply for a building permit. In 2019, the City of San Jose started a preapproved ADU program and approved its first ADU, a 500 square-foot prefab ADU designed by Abodu. This modern-looking ADU costs $199,000 and can be purchased and installed in as little as two weeks.[3]

One potential hurdle to overcome with a modular or manufactured ADU is sufficient side yard access to move the ADU into the backyard. If there is insufficient side-yard access, then a crane would have to be used to drop the ADU into the backyard. At an ADU seminar in May 2019, it was estimated that the total cost of a crane rental in San Jose would be $18,000.[4]

Hiring an Architect / Designer

If the homeowner does not purchase a predesigned ADU model, then it will be necessary to work with an architect or designer to create an ADU. The architect typically uses CAD (computer aided design) software to produce different types of drawings, including:[5]

- Site plan: a map of the homeowner's property that shows the location of the buildings (See Figure 1). Also, the architect provides a site analysis, which includes information about the size of the lot and house, setbacks, and lot coverage.
- Exterior elevations: views of the house from four different sides. See Figure 2 for the exterior elevation of the back of our house, with the in-law unit on the first floor.
- Floor plan: a drawing that shows the layout of one floor of a house from above. (See Chapter 6 for the floor plan of our in-law unit)
- Electrical and lighting plan: a version of the floor plan that shows the location of the electrical outlets and lighting fixtures.

(49)

Figure 1: Site Plan

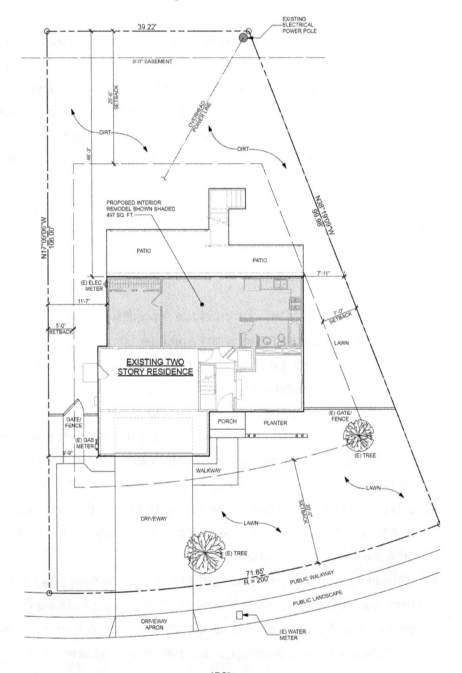

Figure 2: Rear Exterior Elevation

PROPOSED REAR EXTERIOR ELEVATION
Scale: 1/4" = 1'-0"

When looking for a person or company to design an in-law unit, here are some suggestions for the homeowner:

- Ask to see some drawings and pictures of their work. I wish that we had asked our interior designer to show us some architectural drawings prior to signing a contract!
- Ask if they can create interior elevations.[6] Because these perspectives show the interior space with cabinets, appliances, and furniture, they give the homeowner a good feel for how their new space will turn out. Some architects may not be able to create interior elevations.

- Evaluate if they have the skills for designing for an ADU. In-law units are typically small, so it is beneficial if the architect has experience with tighter spaces. This will be discussed more in Chapter 6.
- Ask if the architect has gone through the permit process with the homeowner's local government. If the architect has done work on an ADU project in the homeowner's area, the architect should be aware of the laws that would affect an ADU project.

Hiring a Contractor

In general, our contractor did an excellent job on our ADU. It took a little over four months to build our ADU after we received a permit. Our contractor helped us to save money on our ADU by recommending stores where we could buy good quality finishes at a reasonable price (See Chapter 7). However, in between the time when we finished our ADU and we began the extension and remodeling of our main house, something dramatically changed with our contractor. Our second project with the contractor moved very slowly, and we became very frustrated at different times during the project. What was supposed to be a six-month project dragged out to over a year. At the time I am writing this, it has been 15 months since the beginning of the project and it still isn't finished! We found out that our contractor has not been honest with us. In some cases, the work was not progressing because he did not pay certain subcontractors after we paid the contractor for the work. One subcontractor was surprised about the way our contractor was acting because they had a good business relationship for a long time. Finally, we terminated our contract with the contractor and filed a complaint with the Contractors State License Board (CSLB).

Although I did some research about our contractor before signing a contract with him, I could have done more. I recommend that homeowners read a CSLB pamphlet titled "What You Should Know Before Hiring A Contractor" (www.cslb.ca.gov/Resources/ GuidesAndPublications/ WYSKPamphlet.pdf). This pamphlet contains a lot of helpful information that can save the homeowner a lot of headaches.

It's a good idea to start looking for a contractor at the beginning of the project, even if the ADU has not been designed yet. It is important to get the contractor involved early because the homeowner can get feedback from the contractor about the cost of an ADU design. If the homeowner is working with a design-build firm, then the firm can provide upfront information about the cost of the ADU. However, if the homeowner is working with an architect and contractor that do not work for the same company, then the construction cost of an architect's design is unknown until the contractor evaluates it. Certain designs are less expensive than others. For example, the location of the kitchen and bathrooms can have a significant impact on remodeling costs. Our home, like many houses in California, was built on a slab foundation. The water and sewage lines run under the concrete slab to the different locations in the house where they are needed. During a remodeling project, if a homeowner decides to add or move a bathroom within the existing home, the contractor will have to jackhammer out sections of the concrete slab in order to run the water and sewage lines to the bathroom. Then, the contractor needs to pour new concrete to fill in the holes in the slab. If the contractor needs to remove and replace large sections of concrete, it can be quite expensive. On the other hand, if the new bathroom is located close to the existing water and sewage lines, then the cost will be less. The next chapter covers other issues to consider when designing an ADU.

(Chapter 5 Endnotes)

[1] John DL Arendsen, "There Is Difference Between a HUD Manufactured Home and a Modular Home," August 4, 2017, https://activerain.com/blogsview/5094518/there-is-difference-between-a-hud-manufactured-home---a-modular-home

[2] Kol Peterson, "Manufactured Homes as ADUs and Insights into the Prefab ADU Business Model." August 20, 2018, https://www.buildinganadu.com/adu-blog/manufactured-homes-as-adus.

[3] Liz Stinson, "Sleek Prefab Cabins Adapted into Pre-approved ADUs," Curbed, September 12, 2019. https://www.curbed.com/2019/9/12/20861476/koto-prefab-homes-adu-abodu-san-jose.

[4] Steve Vallejos (2019, May). Small Homes, Big Impact: South County ADU Workshop, Morgan Hill, CA.

[5] Wikipedia, "Architectural Drawing." https://en.wikipedia.org/wiki/Architectural_drawing. Accessed April 3, 2018.

[6] Maxable, "How to Hire an Architect to Design an ADU," https://maxablespace.com/how-to-hire-an-architect-to-design-an-adu/, Accessed November 28, 2019.

We envisioned that our in-law unit would be a fully equipped one-bedroom apartment with a kitchen, bathroom, living room and bedroom, as well as laundry facilities. All of this would have to fit in a space with just under 500 square feet, which was how much room was available in the back part of the first floor (See Figure 3). After the interior design company met with us and understood our needs, they presented us with a couple of options for the floor plan. We liked one design, except that it had the stacked washer/dryer in the bedroom. We asked our interior designer to move the washer/dryer to the bathroom, and she placed the washer/dryer just inside the entrance to the bathroom to the right of the door. There was still enough room in the bathroom for a small vanity, toilet, and walk-in bathtub (See Figure 4).

After we went through the difficult process of getting a permit, our contractor began to construct the in-law unit. After the construction workers had built the framing for the walls for the bathroom, I suspected that there was going to be a problem with the washer/dryer. I took a measurement of our washer/dryer and the area in the bathroom, and it became apparent to me that the stacked washer/dryer would stick out too far and partially block the entrance to the bathroom. I spoke to our contractor and one of his main workers on the project, and we tried to figure out a solution to the problem. We agreed that it would be best to move the door to the wall between the kitchen and the bathroom (See Figure 5).

Figure 3: First Floor Before Remodeling

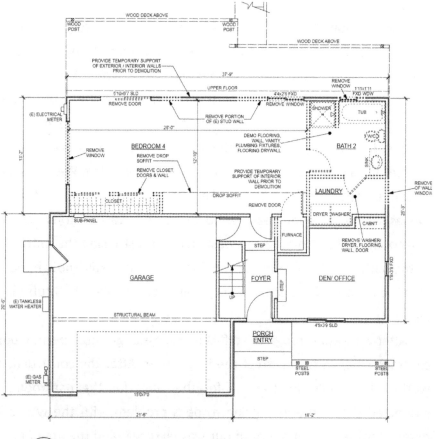

EXISTING LOWER FLOOR - DEMOLITON PLAN
Scale: 1/4" = 1'-0"

Figure 4: First Floor with In-Law Unit (Original Design)

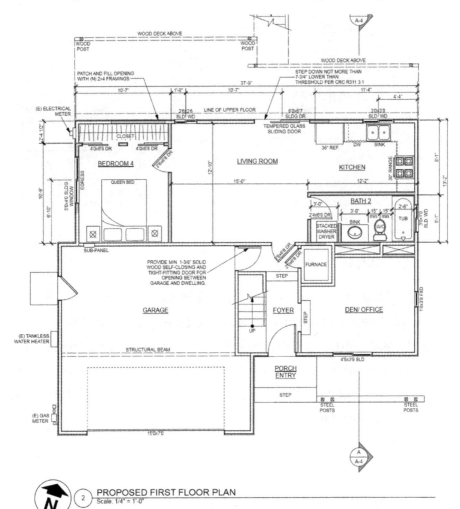

PROPOSED FIRST FLOOR PLAN
Scale: 1/4" = 1'-0"

Figure 5: First Floor with In-Law Unit (Revised Design)

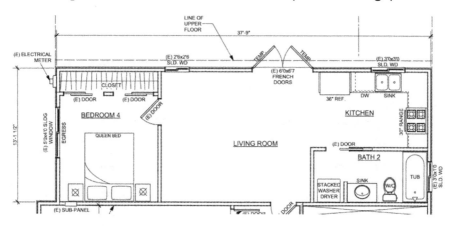

Design Features for an ADU

Designing an in-law unit has some challenges because typically there is not a lot of space to work with. It is beneficial for the homeowner to be familiar with some design ideas for ADUs. One good resource is a free e-Book titled "10 ADU Design Principles" that is available on the website www.buildinganadu.com. Here are some design features that were incorporated into our in-law unit:

• Pocket doors

When we moved the door for the bathroom, we also decided to change from a swinging door to a pocket door. A pocket door is a great space saver because it slides into the wall, and it doesn't require the clearance space that a swinging door does. However, it costs more to install a pocket door than a swinging door. We paid an additional $500 to install the pocket door for the bathroom.

- Open concept

Open-concept floor plans are currently very popular in the design of single-family homes. ADU designers also make use of open-concept floor plans. Kol Peterson writes, "When limited to a small space, it is critical to spatially join the kitchen, living room, and dining room into one great room to create a psychological sense of larger space, as well (as) to leverage additional functionality by overlapping them."[1]

- French doors

It is common for in-law units to face the backyard of a house. We decided to install French doors in order to bring light into the in-law unit and give my mother a nice view of the backyard, where there are many fruit trees.

- Separate heating and air conditioning

It is beneficial to have a separate heating and air conditioning system for the in-law unit, so that the occupant can have control over the temperature in the ADU. We decided to install a wall-mounted heater/air conditioner for the in-law unit

- Walk-in bathtub

Many residents of in-law units will be elderly, so a walk-in bathtub is a nice feature to have. However, when designing the bathroom, make sure to consider where the door to the bathtub is located. We purchased a bathtub with the door on the right side of the tub, close to where the toilet is located (See Figure 5). Unfortunately, after the bathtub and toilet were installed, we found out that there was not enough room to walk in and out of the tub. Fortunately, there was enough space to move the toilet slightly towards the vanity.

In the last chapter, it was mentioned that if the house is built on a slab foundation, it saves money if the location of the new kitchen and bathrooms is close to existing water and sewage lines. Note that in Figures 3 and 4, the new kitchen and bathroom are not far from where the old bathroom was located. As a result, the construction workers only had to jackhammer out a little concrete in order to install the new water and sewage lines. This made the construction a little less expensive. In the next chapter, we will consider other ways to save money on the construction of an in-law unit.

(Chapter 6 Endnotes)

[1] Peterson, *Backdoor Revolution*, 77.

The more that we found out about our home, the more that we realized that it was a fixer upper. When the construction workers did demolition work and opened the walls, they found some old pipes with asbestos that needed to be removed. Also, the electrical system was clearly outdated and needed upgrading. Our contractor gave us a quote of about $46,500 for the work needed to complete the in-law unit. In addition to the contractor fees, we would have to pay for permit fees, a new electrical panel, and an air conditioner/heater. The costs were quickly adding up.

At about the same time, we met with our interior designer, who gave us a proposed budget of over $30,000 for all the finishes (cabinets, countertop, tile, appliances, etc.). After adding up the contractor fees and other costs, we realized that we could not afford to spend that much money on finishes if we wanted to renovate the rest of the house. Therefore, we began to look for ways to save money. Our contractor had mentioned that he knew of places where we could buy finishes at reasonable prices. We asked him for the contact information of a local retailer that sold kitchen cabinets. We found out that the store sold quality white Shaker cabinets that were about one third of the cost of similar cabinets that our interior designer had recommended. We were amazed! Therefore, instead of working with our interior designer to purchase items, we began to ask our contractor where to buy them.

I created an Excel spreadsheet with a detailed budget and monitored our purchases to make sure that we did not overspend. Although we had some additional contractor costs due to some problems with the house, we saved a lot of money on finishes and spent just under $100,000 on the in-law unit. Figure 6 shows our spending for the in-law unit divided into major categories of expenditures. There is also a column that a homeowner can use to make a budget.

Figure 6: Budget for an ADU Project

	Our Spending	Your Budget
Architecture / Designer Fees	$ 3,900	
Structural Engineering	$ 0	
Permit Fees	$ 5,200	
Impact Fees	$ 0	
Construction Insurance	$ 0	
Utility Hookup Fees	$ 0	
Contractor Fees	$ 46,500	
Additional Contractor Fees	$ 9,800	
Air Conditioner / Heater	$ 3,600	
Electrical Panel	$ 2,800	
Finishes	$ 14,000	
Parking Spaces	$ 0	
Landscaping	$ 14,100	
Total	$ 99,900	

Budgeting for Building an ADU

We finished building our ADU before the tariffs on imports from China began in 2018. We saved money by purchasing cabinets from a company that imported products from China. When we purchased cabinets from the same company for the remodeling of our house in 2019, we found that because of the tariffs, the prices had increased significantly. The California Building Industry Association estimates that the tariffs have increased the cost of an average-size new home by $20,000 to $30,000.[1] The impact of the tariffs on an ADU is smaller, but still significant. A homeowner who is building an ADU would be wise to take the tariffs into account when creating a budget.

Here is some information for each expenditure category that a homeowner can use to develop a budget like the one shown in Figure 6:

- Designer / Architecture Fees

Architecture or designer fees vary depending on the type and size of ADU that is being built. A homeowner who is building a newly designed detached cottage can expect to pay higher architecture fees than for a JADU. For a prefabricated or manufactured ADU, the cost of the architecture fees may be included in the total cost of the ADU.

- Structural Engineering

We didn't need to hire a structural engineer for our in-law unit because our ADU was built within the walls of our existing house. However, for any other type of ADU, the homeowner will likely need to hire a structural engineer. The structural engineering costs will depend on the scope of the project. For the extension and remodeling of our main house, we paid $4500 for structural engineering fees.

- Permit Fees

Permit fees from local governments are expensive! I was surprised that we had to pay over $5000 to get a permit from the City of Fremont to build the in-law unit. In the City of Fremont, the base fee depends on the value of the project work. Then, additional fees are added for the planning department approval, plan checking and the different types of inspections. Many cities have their fees listed online, and the City of Los Angeles even has an online permit fee calculator that a homeowner can use to estimate permit fees (https://www.ladbs.org/services/pay-fees/permit-fee-calculator).

- Impact Fees

We avoided having to pay impact fees because the City of Fremont had eliminated impact fees for ADU construction. Although other cities may charge impact fees for ADUs, the 2020 ADU laws prohibit impact fees for ADUs less than 750 square feet.

- Construction Insurance

I contacted my insurance agent, who told me that I did not need any additional insurance for the construction of the JADU and extension. However, if a homeowner is building a detached ADU, it is likely that construction insurance will be necessary. Homeowners who are building an ADU should contact their insurance company before proceeding with the construction.

- Utility Hookup Fees

We didn't have to pay for any utility hookup fees because a JADU is exempt from paying these fees. A homeowner may have to pay these fees depending on the type of ADU being built and the local laws. See Chapter 2 for more information.

- Contractor Fees

The homeowner should sign a detailed contract that specifies the work the contractor will perform and the construction materials that are included in the price. Any materials that are not included in the contract will have to be purchased by the homeowner. Our contract with our contractor included the following work and construction materials:

- ☐ Demolition
- ☐ Debris removal
- ☐ Wall framing
- ☐ Electrical wiring
- ☐ HVAC installation and asbestos abatement
- ☐ Sheetrock and wall texturing
- ☐ Insulation
- ☐ Exterior doors, windows and trim
- ☐ Flooring installation (materials not included)
- ☐ Kitchen installation (materials not included)
- ☐ Bathroom installation (materials not included)
- ☐ Plumbing – including new tankless water heater
- ☐ Painting – exterior and interior (interior paint not included)

In addition, if the homeowner is building a detached cottage, there will be additional costs for the foundation and roofing. Starting in 2020, roofing will be more expensive for homeowners who are building a detached ADU because of the new law in California that requires new homes to have solar panels.

• Additional Contractor Fees

It is a good idea to put some money in the budget for construction cost overruns because the contractor will likely uncover some problems during demolition and construction. It is recommended that the homeowner put at least 10% of the contractor fees in the budget for additional contractor costs. We ended up paying our contractor an additional $9800, which is 21% of the original contractor fee ($46,500). Here are some of the problems that we found during demolition and construction:

☐ A previous owner had installed a stained-glass window incorrectly and as a result, water got into the wall framing and weakened some 2x4 framing studs that held up the house. (The stained-glass window is shown in the first photograph in Figure 7.) The construction workers had to replace not only the framing studs, but also the stucco in that area of the house.

Figure 7

The Area of the Future ADU Bedroom After Wall and Ceiling Demolition

The Area of the Future ADU Bedroom After Wall Framing

☐ When the City of Fremont did a shear inspection of the walls of the in-law unit, they decided that our walls need to be strengthened. We were required to reinforce the walls by using rods that would be anchored in the concrete by epoxy. This work, which also required a special inspection, cost more than $6000.

- Air conditioner / heater

As mentioned in Chapter 6, we decided to have a separate air conditioner / heater for the in-law unit. Our contractor installed a $3600 wall-mounted air conditioner / heater on the wall between the bathroom and the living room.

- Electrical Panel

If a homeowner has a 100-amp electrical panel and is adding an in-law unit, it is almost certain that an upgrade to a 200-amp panel will be required to meet the increased need for electricity. The cost of our new electrical panel was $2800.

- Finishes

See the section later in this chapter.

- Parking Spaces

We didn't have to add any parking spaces on our lot because we built a junior accessory dwelling unit (JADU). However, depending on the type of ADU being built and the local laws, a homeowner may be required to build new parking spaces. See Chapter 2 for more information.

- Landscaping

When budgeting for an in-law unit, it is important to not overlook landscaping, which can be quite expensive. The concrete path to our in-law unit and the concrete patio outside our in-law unit were in poor condition, so we decided to replace them. It cost over $13,000 to remove the old concrete and pour new concrete.

Financing

One barrier to building an ADU has been a lack of financing options. However, as the demand for ADUs has grown in California, more financing options are becoming available. Here are some different options for a homeowner who needs financing for an ADU project:

- Home Equity Line of Credit or Cash-out Refinance

If a homeowner has a lot of equity in their home, then it is possible to get a home equity line of credit (HELOC) or a cash-out refinance. Typically, this is the type of financing offered by large national banks.

- Construction Loan

Some regional banks and credit unions offer construction loans for ADU projects. With a construction loan, homeowners can borrow against the appraised future value of the ADU. One bank to consider is Umpqua Bank, which is based in Portland, but has branches in many different locations in California.

- Vendor Financing

Some builders of prefabricated and manufactured ADUs offer financing for the purchase of their homes.

- Financing from a Non-profit

Increasingly, the non-profit sector is offering loans to homeowners who want to build an ADU. Here are some funding possibilities from non-profits:

- In 2017, JPMorgan Chase awarded a $3.5 million grant to be split among two non-profits—Housing Trust Silicon Valley in Northern California and Genesis LA Economic Development Corp. in Southern California.[2] These funds are to be used to make loans to low income homeowners who want to build an ADU.
- An urban-design non-profit in Los Angeles named LA Más has started the Backyard Homes Project, which offers optional financing to homeowners who want to build an ADU and are willing to rent the ADU to a Section 8 tenant for a minimum of five years.[3]
- On November 27, 2019, the California Department of Housing and Community Development announced the availability of approximately $57 million in state CalHome Program funds,

which may be used for the construction or rehabilitation of ADUs.[4] Non-profits and local governments can apply to receive a portion of these funds for an ADU loan program. Homeowners who have a household income of less than 80 percent of the Area Median Income can qualify for a loan of up to $100,000. Homeowners can check to see if a non-profit or local government in their area offers a loan program from the CalHome Program funds.

Saving Money on Finishes

A homeowner can save money on finishes for an ADU by spending time to do research and to find low-cost retailers for the different types of finishes. If a homeowner does not know where to shop, it is a good idea to ask their contractor or other people who have done remodeling projects. The general strategy that worked the best for us was to ask our contractor where to shop, and then in certain cases, have our interior designer help us to choose the right design and color for our ADU.

When shopping for finishes, it is important to make sure that products comply with the California Green Building Standards Code[5] and the Building Energy Efficiency Standards.[6] California has more stringent requirements than other states on certain plumbing, lighting and ventilation products. Here are the requirements for some of these products:

- ☐ Toilets—maximum of 1.28 gallons per flush
- ☐ Showerheads—maximum of 1.8 gallons per minute
- ☐ Bathroom faucets—maximum of 1.2 gallons per minute

☐ Kitchen faucets—maximum of 1.8 gallons per minute (may temporarily increase to 2.2 gallons per minute)
☐ Bathroom exhaust fans—must have a moisture sensor (humidity control)
☐ Bathroom lights – must have at least one light that is controlled by an occupancy sensor.

Figure 8 shows our spending for finishes divided into major categories of expenditures. There is also a column that a homeowner can use to make a budget.

Figure 8: Budget for Finishes

	Our Spending	Your Budget
Kitchen Cabinets	$ 2,400	
Kitchen Countertop / Sink / Faucet	$ 1,000	
Other Kitchen Finishes	$ 200	
Bathtub	$ 3,700	
Bathroom Vanity / Sink / Faucet	$ 400	
Other Bathroom Finishes	$ 600	
Appliances	$ 1,600	
Flooring	$ 1,700	
Interior Doors / Baseboards	$ 800	
Closet	$ 1,000	
Light Fixtures	$ 400	
Window Treatments	$ 200	
Total	$ 14,000	

- Kitchen Cabinets

We bought the kitchen cabinets that were mentioned at the beginning of this chapter and saved over $5000. The cabinets are well built with the doors, drawers, and frames made of solid wood, and the boxes made of plywood. Also, the cabinets have soft-closing drawers and doors. Our interior designer agreed that these kitchen cabinets are high quality. Because of the tariffs on China imports, it would be difficult to get such a bargain. However, it is still possible to save money on kitchen cabinets.

- Kitchen Countertop / Sink / Faucet

It is also possible to save a lot of money on a kitchen countertop. Our contractor told us about a retailer that has a large warehouse with a big selection of countertop. We found a nice quartz countertop at a very reasonable price and purchased two 10-foot slabs. In addition, we found a nice stainless-steel sink at a discounted price. On top of the reasonable prices, we were able to get a contractor's discount. After purchasing a Hansgrohe faucet on sale at Costco, the total cost for the countertop, sink and faucet was only about $1,000.

- Other Kitchen Finishes

To complete the finishes needed for the kitchen, we purchased backsplash tile from a local tile retailer for under $3.00 a square foot and a garbage disposer on sale at Costco.

- Bathtub

Our contractor recommended that we visit a local retailer that specializes in bathtubs. Walk-in bathtubs are generally very expensive, so we decided to purchase a floor model in order to save money. However, we still had to spend $3,700 for the tub and the fixtures.

- Bathroom Vanity / Sink / Faucet

We decided that we wanted the vanity area of the bathroom to have a similar look as the kitchen. Therefore, we purchased a bathroom vanity at the retailer where we purchased kitchen cabinets. Also, we used the leftover countertop from the kitchen for the bathroom countertop and backsplash. After buying a low-cost sink from the countertop retailer and a Hansgrohe faucet from Costco, our costs to furnish this area of the bathroom were only about $400.

- Other Bathroom Finishes

To complete the bathroom, we purchased a medicine cabinet, toilet, towel bars, fan, shelves and bathtub tile. We bought many of these items from Home Depot. We purchased the bathtub tile for $2.49 per square foot from the discount section of a tile retailer.

- Appliances

Our cost for appliances was rather low because we already had a washer/dryer that we could use in the in-law unit. In addition, we decided to move the dishwasher from the main house's kitchen to the in-law unit. For the refrigerator, stove and microwave, I searched online for sales at Lowe's and used coupons to lower the price even further.

- Flooring

Our interior designer recommended that we purchase luxury vinyl flooring, which is waterproof because it is made of PVC. Our contractor brought us to a flooring distributor that is not open to the public, and we were able to purchase luxury vinyl flooring with padding for $2.99 per square foot. We chose a type of luxury vinyl flooring that looks like wood and asked our contractor to install it in all areas of the in-law unit, including the bathroom.

- Interior Doors / Baseboards

We found that doors are rather expensive. We went to a door retailer that our contractor recommended and purchased three interior doors and baseboard for about $800.

- Closet

Because in-law units are small, there is typically limited storage space available. In our ADU, only the bedroom has a closet, which is about ten feet long (See Figure 3 in Chapter 6). We decided to install a custom closet system in order to maximize the storage space. Although this system was rather costly, we feel that it was worth the cost. The closet has two different sections, so we had to purchase four sliding doors. We ended up spending about $1,000 on the closet and doors.

- Light Fixtures

Our contractor installed recessed lighting in every room of the in-law unit, so we didn't have to purchase many light fixtures. We purchased a bathroom light fixture and three sconces for the living room.

- Window Treatments

We decided not purchase window treatments for the French doors and window in the living room in order to let more natural light into the ADU. We purchased wood blinds for the bedroom and curtains for the kitchen.

Although it took a lot of work to purchase all the finishes, it was worth it because we were able to keep our spending on finishes close to our budget. Also, we were able to get good quality items that made our ADU look nice.

(Chapter 7 Endnotes)

[1] Kate Irby, "Trump's Tariffs Made California's Housing Crisis Worse: A 'Perfect Storm of the Wrong Kind'," Sacramento Bee, September 5, 2019, https://www.sacbee.com/news/business/article234699897.html.

[2] Allison Bisby, "In Tight Housing Market, Lenders Get Creative to Finance Garage Apartments," Asset Securitization Report, November 16, 2018. asreport.americanbanker.com/news/in-tight-housing-market-lenders-get-creative-to-finance-garage-apartments.

[3] LA Más, The Backyard Homes Project, https://www.mas.la/affordable-adus. Accessed December 9, 2019.

[4] California Department of Housing and Community Development, CalHome Program Notice of Funding Availability, November 27, 2019. https://www.hcd.ca.gov/grants-funding/active-no-funding/calhome/docs/CalHome%202019%20General%20NOFA.pdf

[5] California Building Standards Commission, 2019 California Green Building Standards Code. https://codes.iccsafe.org/content/CAGBSC2019/cover

[6] California Energy Commission, 2019 Residential Compliance Manual. https://www.energy.ca.gov/programs-and-topics/programs/building-energy-efficiency-standards/2019-building-energy-efficiency-0

PROJECT MANAGEMENT & PERSEVERANCE

By November 2017, the construction workers had made good progress on our in-law unit, and we were hoping the work would be completed before Thanksgiving. When the texturing of the walls was almost done, our contractor asked us to pick colors for the interior walls so that the house could be painted before the flooring was installed. Our interior designer helped us to choose a few possible colors, and we put some patches of different paint colors on the wall of the in-law unit. We communicated our choices to our contractor, who told us that one of his painting subcontractors would be coming on a particular day to do the work. However, at around 11am on the day that our house was supposed to be painted, I noticed that no one had shown up to work. At this stage in the project, I knew that I should contact our contractor right away and let him know that the painter did not show up. Something like this had happened several times during the project and caused delays. After I texted our contractor, he let me know that the painting subcontractor had not responded to him, so he contacted another painter who would come the next morning. We were pleased that we did not lose much time because this second painter showed up the next morning and completed the work.

The Homeowner is a Project Manager

What we have learned is that although the contractor is overseeing the in-law construction project, the homeowner needs to be very involved in the project management. A contractor usually is overseeing several projects at the same time and is not always on site. Therefore, it is important for the homeowner to have strong involvement in the management of the project so that there will not be lengthy delays. During a project, there is often a sequence of events that needs to occur on a specific part of the renovation project:

- □ The homeowner decides which items to purchase.
- □ The purchases of the items are made ahead of time so that they will be available to install. Sometimes, there is a lead time involved with purchasing a particular item.
- □ The contractor schedules a subcontractor to do the work.
- □ A subcontractor goes to the job site to do the work. Sometimes, the subcontractor needs to ask the homeowner exactly how to install the items.

Here's an example of this process. A long time before the bathroom was constructed, we worked with our interior designer to decide what items to purchase. For the area above the vanity, she recommended that we purchase an oval medicine cabinet and a LED light fixture. I made online purchases of a medicine cabinet from Home Depot and the light fixture from Lowes. The medicine cabinet was delivered to our house in a timely manner. However, the delivery from Lowes was rather slow because the light fixture was a special-order item. Unfortunately, the light fixture did not arrive by the time when the subcontractor began working on the area around the bathroom vanity.

The subcontractor wanted to know exactly where on the wall to install the medicine cabinet and light fixture, but we didn't have the light fixture. He was unable to finish the work in this area until the light fixture arrived later, five weeks after I had ordered it.

During an in-law construction project, a homeowner needs to communicate with many different people. It is almost certain that during the project, a homeowner will find it challenging to work with some of the people. Here are the people with whom a homeowner may interact:

- ☐ Architect / Designer
- ☐ Structural engineer
- ☐ Contractor
- ☐ Subcontractors
- ☐ Vendors
- ☐ Local government employees
- ☐ Utility company employees
- ☐ Family members who will live in the in-law unit

Perseverance

At the beginning of each episode of *Fixer Upper* on HGTV, Joanna Gaines says, "Do you have the guts to take on a fixer upper?" This question is a good one for a homeowner to consider because a renovation project takes a lot of patience and perseverance. Although *Fixer Upper* is an entertaining program and shows viewers some of the challenges they will face, I don't think that it provides a true representation of what most homeowners in California will encounter during an in-law construction project. *Fixer Upper* does not show the challenges of getting permits from the local government. Probably, it is much easier to get a building permit in Waco, Texas (where *Fixer Upper* is filmed) than in most places in California. Also, most people will not have the opportunity to hire a talented and dedicated couple like Chip and Joanna Gaines, who can basically handle the entire renovation project—designing, constructing, and decorating—and lighten things up with their humor. It is more likely that a homeowner will have struggles managing the project and working with some people. It may be difficult to keep a sense of humor! We struggled with this as we dealt with problems that were described in earlier chapters. Here are some of the additional difficulties that we faced during our project:

- Redesigning the layout for the main house

While our contractor was building the in-law unit, we worked on the design for the main house, which included a second-floor extension. In Chapter 3, I mentioned the floor area ratio rule that prevented us from doing an extension to the second floor. We really wanted to have more room on the second floor so that we could have two bedrooms and two bathrooms. After consulting with our architect, we decided to do a small extension at the front of our house. The garage and piano room would be enlarged and a restroom for the piano students would be added. In addition, the entrance would be moved forward, which would allow us to also move the staircase forward towards the front of the house. This would give us a little more room on the second floor, and we would be able to squeeze in two bedrooms and two bathrooms.

- Getting a permit for the main house

In Chapter 4, I wrote about how difficult it was to get a permit for the in-law unit. While the work on the in-law unit was being completed, we began to work on getting a permit for the main house so that we could start work on the main house as soon as the in-law unit was completed. Unfortunately, getting a second permit from the City of Fremont was not any easier than getting the first permit. The process continued long after the in-law unit was finished. First, the project was delayed because our architect was not available to work for quite a long time. Then, we ran into issues with the City of Fremont. When we applied for the permit for the main house, a plan checker from the City of Fremont told us that we could not have two permits open at the same time. Our contractor tried to convince him that he was wrong because there were two different units (the in-law unit and the main house) but was unsuccessful in changing the plan checker's mind. We changed our application to make it a revision of the in-law unit permit and submitted it. Then, another City of Fremont employee contacted us. She apologized and told us that we had received bad information from the plan checker and that we had to apply for a separate permit for the main house. This mistake by the plan checker cost us three weeks of time.

After we submitted our application to the City of Fremont, we received a comment back by a plan examiner who stated that we had to install automatic sprinklers because our renovation was considered new construction. After checking our plan, he concluded that over 50% of our interior walls were being replaced, and according to a section of the Fremont Municipal Code, this made our renovation to be considered new construction. We definitely didn't want to spend money on a costly sprinkler system, so I checked the code to see if we really had to install sprinklers. I found that the plan examiner did not apply the code correctly. A renovation is considered new construction if both the following conditions apply:

- ☐ 50% of the interior and exterior walls are replaced.
- ☐ 50% of the roof is replaced.

Since we would not be replacing 50 percent of the roof nor 50 percent of the exterior walls, our renovation would not be considered new construction, and we wouldn't have to install a sprinkler system.

The lesson that we learned is that when a local government employee says that something is required or not allowed, the homeowner should ask to see the law in writing and make sure that the employee is interpreting the law correctly. I would expect that the local government employees would know how to apply the laws correctly, but I found that this is not always the case. Respectfully questioning the local government employees may save the homeowner a lot of time and money.

A Happy Ending

We were hoping to move into the in-law unit before Thanksgiving 2017, but some construction delays forced us to continue to live in the main house, which was quite chilly because the furnace had been removed during the in-law construction. We endured some chilly December days with the help of a space heater as we waited for the construction to be finished. On December 22, our contractor and his workers helped us to move into the in-law unit. We were pleased about how great the in-law unit looked! (See Figure 9)

A couple days later, my mother came to stay with us in the in-law unit for Christmas. My mother had some concerns that the in-law unit would feel too small and cramped. After all, she had been living for over 30 years in a townhouse with 2,400 square feet, and now she was going to live in an ADU with 497 square feet. When she stayed in the in-law unit, she was pleasantly surprised that the space was comfortable. She really loved the in-law unit and was very excited about living there in the future. When I saw how excited my mother was, I felt that all the struggles and delays that we had gone through were worth it. We now have a beautiful in-law unit which my mother can enjoy and call home.

Figure 9
The Kitchen

The Living Room

The Bathroom

Arendsen, John DL, "There Is Difference Between a HUD Manufactured Home and a Modular Home," August 4, 2017. https://activerain.com/blogsview/5094518/there-is-difference-between-a-hud-manufactured-home---a-modular-home.

Behzadiari, Shila, (2019, May 17). ADUs: Not Just for Granny Anymore, Seminar sponsored by AARP and Housing Trust Silicon Valley, San Jose, CA.

Bisby, Allison, "In Tight Housing Market, Lenders Get Creative to Finance Garage Apartments," Asset Securitization Report, November 16, 2018. asreport.americanbanker.com/news/in-tight-housing-market-lenders-get-creative-to-finance-garage-apartments.

Blomquist, Daren "The Promise and Pitfalls of ADUs as Affordable Housing Panacea," Attom Data Solutions, April 6, 2018. https://www.attomdata.com/news/affordability/promise-pitfalls-adus-affordable-housing-panacea/

California Building Standards Commission, 2019 California Green Building Standards Code. https://codes.iccsafe.org/content/CAGBSC2019/cover

California Department of Housing and Community Development, "Accessory Dwelling Unit Memorandum," December 2018. https://www.hcd.ca.gov/policy-research/docs/ADU-TA-Memorandum.pdf.

California Department of Housing and Community Development, CalHome Program

Notice of Funding Availability, November 27, 2019. https://

www.hcd.ca.gov/grants-funding/active-no-funding/calhome/docs/
CalHome%202019%20General%20NOFA.pdf.

California Energy Commission, 2019 Residential Compliance
Manual. https://www.energy.ca.gov/programs-and-topics/programs/
building-energy-efficiency-standards/2019-building-energy-
efficiency-0

California Legislative Information, SB-13 Accessory Dwelling Units:
09/13/19 – Senate Floor Analyses, https://leginfo.legislature.ca.gov/
faces/billAnalysisClient.xhtml?bill_id=201920200SB13.

Chapple, Karen, Wegmann, Jake, Mashhood, Farzad and Coleman,
Rebecca, Jumpstarting the Market for Accessory Dwelling Units:
Lessons Learned from Portland, Seattle and Vancouver, Terner Center
for Housing Innovation, UC Berkeley, April 2017.

Chiland, Elijah, "LA Home Prices Inch up to an All-Time High," Curbed
Los Angeles, July 26, 2019. https://la.curbed.com/2019/7/26/8931996/
los-angeles-median-home-price-record-high.

Chilland, Elijah, "Power Lines Preventing LA Homeowners from
Building ADUs," Curbed Los Angeles, November 27, 2018. https://
la.curbed.com/2018/11/27/18069692/los-angeles-adu-construction-
granny-flats-dwp

City of Fremont Community Development Department, "Accessory
Dwelling Units," April 2017. https://fremont.gov/DocumentCenter/
Home/View/4073.

Fry, Richard, "For First Time in Modern Era, Living with Parents
Edges Out Other Living Arrangements for 18- to 34-Year-Olds," Pew
Research Center, May 24, 2016.

www.pewsocialtrends.org/2016/05/24/for-first-time-in-modern-
era-living-with-parents-edges-out-other-living-arrangements-for-18-
to-34-year-olds/

Garcia, David, "ADU Update: Early Lessons and Impacts of
California's State and Local Policy Changes," Terner Center for Housing
Innovation, UC Berkeley, December 21, 2017.

https://ternercenter.berkeley.edu/blog/adu-update-early-lessons-and-impacts-of-californias-state-and-local-policy

Irby, Kate, "Trump's Tariffs Made California's Housing Crisis Worse: A 'Perfect Storm of the Wrong Kind'," Sacramento Bee, September 5, 2019, https://www.sacbee.com/news/business/article234699897.html.

LA Más, The Backyard Homes Project, https://www.mas.la/affordable-adus. Accessed December 9, 2019.

Litchfield, Michael. *In-Laws, Outlaws, and Granny Flats*. Newtown, CT: The Taunton Press, 2011.

Los Angeles City Planning Department Quarterly Newsletter, Summer 2019, 11. https://planning.lacity.org/odocument/c677b589-a30e-4fb9-a614-000c39e308ab/2019_SUMMER.pdf

Los Angeles County Department of Regional Planning, "An Ordinance Amending Title 22 (Planning and Zoning) of the Los Angeles County Code Related to Accessory Dwelling Units," http://planning.lacounty.gov/assets/upl/case/2017-004091_attachmentC-20180124.pdf. Accessed March 12, 2018.

Los Angeles Department of Water & Power, Pole Spotter Flyer, https://www.ladwp.com/ladwp/faces/ladwp/partners/p-constructionservices/p-cs-electricservices/p-cs-es-constructionnearpowerlines?_adf.ctrl-state=pqgxj3f5_834. Accessed December 4, 2019.

Maxable, "How to Hire an Architect to Design an ADU." https://maxablespace.com/how-to-hire-an-architect-to-design-an-adu/. Accessed November 28, 2019.

McLaughlin, Katy, "The Hottest Home Amenity: In-Law Apartments," *The Wall Street Journal*, November 6, 2014. https://www.wsj.com/articles/the-hottest-home-amenity-in-law-apartments-1415288579

Mortice, Zach, "A One-Stop Shop for Affordable Backyard Homes Advances in L.A.," Citylab, May 1, 2019. https://www.citylab.com/design/2019/05/backyard-homes-los-angeles-affordable-housing-section-8-adu/588370/

National Association of Realtors, "Buyers Value Storage Space, In-Law Suites, NAR Survey Finds," March 13, 2013. https://www.nar.realtor/newsroom/buyers-value-storage-space-in-law-suites-nar-survey-finds

Orange County Register Editorial Board, "Rising Rents a Symptom of California's Housing Crisis," *Orange County Register*, October 17, 2017. https://www.ocregister.com/2017/10/17/rising-rents-a-symptom-of-californias-housing-crisis/

Pender, Kathleen, "New California Housing Laws Make Granny Units Easier to Build," *San Francisco Chronicle*, December 3, 2016. https://www.sfchronicle.com/news/article/New-California-housing-laws-make-granny-units-10688483.php

Peterson, Kol. *Backdoor Revolution: The Definitive Guide to ADU Development*. Portland: Accessory Dwelling Strategies, LLC, 2018.

Peterson, Kol, "Manufactured Homes as ADUs and Insights into the Prefab ADU Business Model." August 20, 2018. https://www.buildinganadu.com/adu-blog/manufactured-homes-as-adus.

Rent Jungle, "Rent Trend Data in Los Angeles, California." https://www.rentjungle.com/average-rent-in-los-angeles-rent-trends/. Accessed November 9, 2019.

Rent Jungle, "Rent Trend Data in San Francisco, California." https://www.rentjungle.com/average-rent-in-san-francisco-rent-trends/. Accessed November 9, 2019.

Semuels, Alana, "Little Homes in Big Backyards: San Francisco's Housing Solution?" *The Atlantic*, February 18, 2016. https://www.theatlantic.com/business/archive/2016/02/little-homes-in-big-backyards-san-franciscos-housing-solution/463326/

Stinson, Liz, "Sleek Prefab Cabins Adapted into Pre-approved ADUs," Curbed, September 12, 2019. https://www.curbed.com/2019/9/12/20861476/koto-prefab-homes-adu-abodu-san-jose.

Terner Center for Housing Innovation, UC Berkeley, Residential Impact Fees in California, August 5, 2019.

Vallejos, Steve, (2019, May 4), Small Homes, Big Impact: South County ADU Workshop, Sponsored by Housing Trust Silicon Valley, Morgan Hill, CA.

Wieckowski, Bob, (2019, May 17), ADUs: Not Just for Granny Anymore, Seminar sponsored by AARP and Housing Trust Silicon Valley, San Jose, CA.

Wikipedia, "Architectural Drawing." https://en.wikipedia.org/wiki/Architectural_drawing. Accessed April 3, 2018.

Zillow.com. "Fremont Home Prices & Values," https://www.zillow.com/fremont-ca/home-values. Accessed November 7, 2019.

CPSIA information can be obtained
at www.ICGtesting.com
Printed in the USA
LVHW010242260620
658994LV00013B/1782